Now Let's Get Brunch:

A Collection of RuPaul's Drag Race Twitter Poetry

Now Let's Get Brunch:
A Collection of
RuPaul's Drag Race
Twitter Poetry

Alex Carrigan

QUERENCIA

Querencia Press, LLC
Chicago Illinois

QUERENCIA PRESS

© Copyright 2023
Alex Carrigan

ISBN 978 1 959118 27 5

www.querenciapress.com

First Published in 2023

Querencia Press, LLC
Chicago IL

Printed & Bound in the United States of America

Every poem in this collection was created from the official Twitter accounts of 40 drag queens who appeared across the RuPaul's Drag Race franchise. The official accounts are cited at the end of each poem.

While some edits have been made to the text, the intent of these lines remains the same.

*This book is dedicated to Rachel Kurasz,
my favorite shady lobster lady.*

Contents

Bob the Drag Queen Gazes Into the Purse, and the Purse Gazes Also

Sometimes I'm like,
"I fucking love the internet,"
and other times I'm like,
"This is the most vapid, disgusting place
I've ever been in my life."

Liberal, woke, social justice TikTok
might be the most toxic, cannibalistic, incestuous
place on the internet.
I had to unfollow all of them.

Antivax Christians are fighting for their lives
in my mentions and I LOVE it.
HAHAHAHA.
You don't believe in the vaccine because
there's not enough proof,
but you fully believe in God. . . okay.
If Jesus was real and came back,
I don't think he would like y'all.

What is going on?
Are you having a stroke?
Who hacked your account?
Next thing we know, you'll be selling PS5s.
Sounds like you ARE the drama.

You love that you're interacting with me.
You're having such a fan moment,
be honest.

You think I'm sharing EVERYTHING?
Baby, you don't wanna see the drafts.
TBH, I always love interacting with fans
and I like fighting so. . .
yes.

Last question:
Does anyone else remember
the brief period in time
when you could make calls on Grindr?
Literally nobody.

So excited to share this with you all.
It's the little things that make a house a home.

Source: @thatonequeen

Kandy Muse Sitting Alone in the Black Lodge

Took an edible, ladies.
I'm having revelations.

Fashion is art and art is subjective.
I can wear the most beautiful outfit in the world
made by the hands of God himself
and people would still be up in arms.

I felt and looked amazing last night,
so the opinions of you and every other
bundle of sticks that wears matching sets
from ASOS really does not matter.

Please stop messaging venues
saying we're cousins so you can get in for free.
Bitch, wait till I get my hands on you.
I mean, c'mon...THAT FACE!
Apology video with tears, NOW.

That's the joke, bitch.
ANOTHER STANDING OVATION!
I'm trying to put the House of Aja back on the map.

Y'all, I've been craving a Korean corn dog
for the longest time now.
No, I've never had them,
but they always look so good.
Am I talking too much,
or are y'all not talking enough?!

Girl, what the hell?
This edible's kicking my ass.
What are we doing today?

Source: @TheKandyMuse

Laganja Estranja Discovers a New Color When the Chronic Hits

Lighten up and smoke a blunt.
The cannabis community deserves/needs this visibility!!
If it ain't green, I ain't interested!!

I love a nice Sativa dab in the morning
before I head to hot yoga!!
I find this not only helps to relax me
but also strengthens my focus in class.
This is TALENT.

Thank you for noticing my hard work!!

I'm just so grateful you consider me a celebrity
bahahaha
but also, so sorry about that,
I am annoying, I know.

You all want the show to be dramatic,
and then when someone provides that—
you hate on them!!
Cry me a river, whore!

Never forget, you are FIERCE
no matter what the judges
in your life say.
Keep being you,
and everything else will fall in place!!
Say it louder!! Yes GAWDDDD!!

I'll never forget this night!!
I told y'all we were going to get sickening...

Source: @LaganjaEstranja

Trinity the Tuck Pumps Up Her Sprit and Her Lips

Good morning, world!
In the words of Faye Dunaway
as Joan Crawford in *Mommy Dearest*:
"Now let's get to work!"

Baby, if you don't got thick skin,
DON'T try out for *Drag Race*.
These kids are NASTY to the girls in the comments.
Haters aren't buying tickets to the shows of people they hate.
They aren't buying merch. They aren't supporting them.

It's completely okay to block toxic
people out of your life,
be it social media or actual reality.
You don't owe anyone who's negative
towards you anything.
It's your life and your mental health,
and if it's better for you, then block away!

Why are you commenting on my shit
when you don't follow me?
Go spread your BS somewhere else.
I swear, y'all come out of the woodwork
just to be negative.
Hate your life elsewhere.
Calm your puss.

Can we as a community stop questioning
how people feel?
That's how THEY feel, and so there isn't
a debate about it.
Life should be a fantasy...reality sucks lol.

Girl, thank Gay God for the block button.
Some of these people are so annoying and so entitled.
No, you don't get to say whatever you want
and then expect anyone to not react to it.

Bitch, you are dumb.
Block!
Don't @ me!
Block!
You are a POS!

Trinity The Block continues...
every person I block, I get younger!
I'm feeling great today!

Source: @TrinityTheTuck

The Vivienne Does a Tip Spot Outside 10 Downing Street

Pro tip: read through the script before choosing roles.
New Prime Minister.
Ugh, why can't somebody cool do it for a change?
So sick of boring, 15 denier-wearing,
beige faced, never-left-London morons
running this country.

Can't Joanna Lumley do it?
We've had enough clowns, thanks!
Wish they'd throw mash potato over Boris.

If you're gonna do a character,
do a character,
not something similar/"this will do."
Commit to your craft.

I'm howling at some of the comments!
I'm a "deviant!"
"Pushing an agenda!"
"Don't let the kids watch!"
"I'll never watch again!"

Well, in the meantime,
turn off *Mrs. Doubtfire*, *White Chicks*,
Mrs. Brown's Boys, and Lily Savage.
Don't go see *Matilda the Musical*.

I'm literally a man in a frock.
An unapologetic masterclass on how to live life!
What's real is people, conversations, laughter, and theatre.
Even if you're doing your own version,
there should be a standard and not laziness.

Oh, this isn't aimed at anyone in particular.
I just see so many performers that do shit half-assed,
when I know what they're earning.
It's so sloppy.
Oh gal, the burns, the glues,
the blisters, if they only knew.
Lol, if you scroll enough you'll see plenty of it!

And who even cares?
Season's been and gone.
I'm off for a Sicilian cappuccino!
Hope I can find one.

Source: @THEVIVIENNEUK

Monet X. Change Records Five Podcasts at Once

A few things to know about me:

I miss Tumblr porn.
My newest tattoo is so beautiful I want to cry.
I left my vape and edibles in Cali.
I will never understand America's
obsession with guns.
Abolish guns.
Just abolish the student fucking loans.
Forever. Always.
It do take nerve.
It is a privilege to be alive in the time of @Zendaya.
I can't wait to get my booster shot.
I popped a pimple today and three more of
dem fuckers showed up to its funeral.
I wish I had kids,
only so they can run back and get shit
I forgot when checking out at the supermarket.
Little children upset and melting into a tantrum
over the slightest inconvenience is always funny to me.
Like, girl, it's a cup of water...
I'll get you another one.

Yo...I'm mad pretty.
I looked great last night.
Thirty, flirty, and thriving.
Acknowledged by the goddess herself!

Normalize telling your friends you love them.
Fully cried at the Issa and Molly
moment from the *Insecure* finale.
Ok, I pretended to understand...
but I'm a fucking idiot and really didn't.
Lmao!

Source: @monetxchange

Farrah Moan Doesn't Emphasize, The Highlights

2022 has been a dumpster fire so far 😊

I hate social media.
I think it's the trauma.
I've seen funnier videos exploiting my trauma.
People really think the only thing that's ever
broken my soul was a slip on television,
as if I couldn't write an entire book
on the situations I've barely survived.

Every time I feel like I'm starting to
climb out of this hole I've been in,
the universe stomps on my fingers
and I fall back down to the bottom.

Kinda ready to leave
my tear-soaked lashes
all over the place.

My point is, it isn't harmless.
And it isn't funny.

Nothing like realizing all
your memories are melting away.
I only have like twelve left.

Secure those therapists immediately.

Until I'm comfortable sharing the magnitude
of what I've been through,
kindly STFU.

I have so much I could say,
but I'mma keep it cute.
That's why whenever I have some time
to sit on my phone, I reply to
as many positive messages and DM's
that I have the mental capacity to.

We better hang out in denim booty shorts
with our thongs hanging out
when I come to Chicago next.
Can't wait to change my hand soaps to
pumpkin flavor and cry to Adele
for the next three months.

Don't forget to take your
Avril Lavigne pills today.
My mom still won't listen to me,
but maybe she'll see this tweet and consider it.

Source: @farrahrized

Mo Heart Sets the Pulpit Alight with Just Her Voice

Hello world, hello America,
happy Sunday.
Say it back.

Y'all remember 2020,
like what were we DOIN?

This is a PSA:
we are not putting any negativity in the world,
and we are here for you too love.

If there were two line items on
this "gay agenda,"
what would they be?

Alexa, play "Bang Bang."

BOUNCE FOR THE KINGDOM.

Bringing some drama
to *iCarly* season 2.
The fairy godmother...
would make an iconic guest.
Don't you just love how straight people
watch queer culture like a hawk and just steal?
I can't with y'all, lmaooo.

Whose closet should we walk out of next?
Come through king!!!!
If you stay yassified,
you don't have to get yassified.

Source: @IAmMoniqueHeart

Shea Couleé Armors Up for Her Next Slaying

I love how in thirty seconds on this app,
I can be incredibly informed,
incredibly entertained,
and incredibly confused.

Some of y'all MF's are too damn smart
on this bird app.
I need a dictionary and thesaurus
just to understand some of y'all's tweets.

Like, I had to look up "neologism"
on a Saturday morning.
I don't even know what's real anymore.
Everything's cake...

I'm tickled when queens who I KNOW
have auditioned for *RPDR* several times
make a point to publicly let everyone
know that they don't watch the show.
The girls really be going for it at the brunch gigs...

And I say this as someone who had to
audition FIVE times to get cast.
There is nothing wrong with rejection.

Success requires determination.
Making your dreams come true
doesn't happen overnight.
It takes hard work,
so roll up them sleeves, gal, and get to it!

You betta let them know, Jackée!!!

Damn, bitch. What a week.
Worked really hard.
But I'm so grateful that I get to wake up
every day and do what I love.
Now let's get brunch...

Source: *@SheaCoulee*

Pandora Boxx
After the Hinges Rust Off

I'm really over people saying shitty things to me and about me.
When people say so-n-so was a bitch or
"I met 'her' and they were not nice" or whatever.
What people seem to leave out is...
WTF did you say to them or how did you treat this queen?!?
Cuz some of you are WAY extra but then go off
saying that queen was terrible. Check. Yo. Self.

Caitlyn Jenner is absolute garbage.
Just when you think she can't
get any worse, she does.
I have also officially cursed that woman
with explosive diarrhea for the rest of 2022.
I have serious questions to ANY woman that
votes for this woman.
Or anyone that does. Trash.

When you are in an Uber and
they are driving questionably,
my only thought is:
please don't make me die in drag on the 101,
which I'll have to haunt FOREVER!!
I need to always wear a long white dress
every time I am in a car in LA though.
It's a better haunting outfit.
Vroom, vroom.

100 people can be in a room and
99 of them could say they hate me.
So I'm like…"Well, I'mma blow that one."
And I would really turn it up.
Haha ohhhh yes!

If you just can't get enough of me:
I really need to get my Dr. Beverly Crusher look
together finally and do a Dr. Crusher drag number.
I. Love. Her.
I can NOT wait!!! So exciting!!!

Source: @ThePandoraBoxx

Kitty Scott-Claus Unites All of Manchester Under a Pink Banner

Manchester!! I'm back!
Guess how many hours I'm here for this time?
Winner wins nothing.

I've just dropped two not-so-subtle clues.
OMG, I feel like Taylor Swift.
I'm in my girl boss era.

If I ever release music my EP,
it would be called "Elaine Paige,"
because that's what it stands for.
My second album would be called
"EP on Sunday" (naturally).

Rushed home, got into drag, and just got
into my Uber to go to brunch,
and the first thing the driver said was "Long night?"

MORNING SWEETHEART,
DIDN'T REALISE WE WERE READING THE GIRLS!

It only seems to be Manchester!
And it breaks my heart cus I love it so much.
I'm available if you want me to model,
but I get it if you don't want to look ugly next to me.
I'm the new Diana. Pass it on.

In true Kitty style, I've been in Manchester
for just over 12 hours, and now I'm on my way
back to London for brunch.
But don't worry Manchester,
I'll be back on Thursday
(for approximately 14 hours).
IM COMING BACK FOR YOU!

Source: @kittyscottclaus

Yuhua Hamasaki Finds a Genuine Designer Bag on a Table Full of Bootlegs

In this Haus, we stan cringe!!!!
Why get the official
when you can get the bootleg
for just as good?

Yes henny,
the first ever FDA-approved local queen!
Yuhua Karen-saki is here to
speak to the manager.
Even though she knows she's in fact the problem.

Reddit knows what's up.

I always get the job done.
I'll rather die trying hard than be unemployed.
Being an adult means being on hold
with customer service for the rest of your life.

If you're not following me on all platforms,
you're only getting half the story!!!
Go leave some positive comments if you can!
OnlyFans and Cameo email me way
much more to join them
than #DragRace wtf yo?

Anyway, who's ready for drag brunch?
Thank you for supporting local drag!!
Just don't show nobody photos
of how I look the next day.

Source: @YuhuaHamasaki

Tia Kofi Might Need to Switch to Matcha

Bonjour, hi!

Fully entered my sexy era.
Welcome to Tia 3.0.
Different dressing gown, same energy.
I need a drag son called "Jamie Dodger" immediately.
In this family, we wear high ponytails.
I'm like a Barbie, I'm gonna party.

Come hang out with your besties
while we talk about queer things.
This week, Tia has opinions.

I've mostly been drinking tea and
watching *Doctor Who* so like…
an ideal night for me!

Is it narcissistic that I'm sat here listening to my own music?
Get ready for this video babes.
This is incredibly impressive work.
Genuinely incredibly talented and wonderful.

Alexa, play "Call Me Mother" by Ruth Paul.

Would you rather have the chaos of a six-way lip sync instead?
This is A-grade content.

Ok, this is camp!
Villain edit tbh.
I blame the Tories.

Source: @TiaKofi

Aquaria Hits Shuffle on Her iPod Nano When the Molly Hits

It's fashion o'clock again...
Does anyone...still turn...a look???
The devil wears Prada...
so the bride of Chucky wore Miu.

Currently in my Maddie Ziegler era.
Pose!! Get done up! Bring a little drama!
Call me, beep me, etc.

Imagine you came to my Xmas show
and all that I performed was
SOPHIE, Rina Sawayama, Kim Petras,
Bree Runway, and Tchaikovsky...
and I made it make sense??

It's a major upgrade from applauding
normality and mediocrity!
Give a lil' something-something in the new year.
Next week better be kooky!!!

Where would Manhattan nightlife be
in this day and age without
The Magician Remix of Lykke Li's "I Follow Rivers"...
not sure it would still be standing!
No one writes music like this anymore and it's so sad.
What a bop.

Praying for minimal discourse following
this upcoming Sunday's Grammy's.
There better be big fights!!!
I need martial arts shows!!!!

Eep, I take it back
They really killed Daft Punk, huh.
Is there a Daft Punk
summoning circle thingy
I can retweet?
Any takers???

Source: @aquariaofficial

Ginger Minj Licks a Glamour Toad and It Gets Weird

Home sick in bed.
It's definitely a thrilla in Manila,
but there's no Diana or Camilla.
I'm still bummed COVID kept me from Pride!

Sometimes I can't sleep, so my mind wanders.
Everything in life seemed to make more sense
once I realized it was "make ends meet"
and not "make ends meat."
I had no idea!

Send dad jokes!
Southern Fried Sass.
I feel like death warmed over.

When I was younger, I showered in the morning
because if I did it right before bed it kept me awake,
but now I've flipped and shower before bed
to make sure there is no glitter or makeup anywhere!
It's fantastic.

Okay, but this is the real tea.
That poor puppeteer will never get his hand back.
I had forgotten how much I really enjoyed it!

Merry Christmas to all who celebrate
and Happy Saturday to those who don't!
I love y'all so much!

Source: @TheGingerMinj

Gottmik Inhales
a Rainbow-Colored Fume

Someone taught me the difference between
tonic water and soda water the other day
and my life has changed.
I literally thought my cocktail just sucked sometimes.

There are too many rules.
I literally don't even have a clock in my kitchen.
Not a fan of that.

Thin brow haters are OUT!
I am insanely shocked.
More cursed than Annabelle.
Don't worry!! I'll stop them!!

I just woke up from a 10-hour nap
by accident, so now I'm just going
to survive.

Update: I fell asleep again
and just woke up so
we loveeee a 17-hour nap.
Oh my god Y E S.

Everyone's gay.
Basically facts if you ask ME.
Relatable queeennnn.

Source: @gottmik

Violet Chachki: Portrait of a Bothered Queen

At a party in Paris,
and all I can think about is how
I am going to have to wash my hair and
dry clean my clothes because everyone smokes indoors.

Thank God we left.
Could you imagine groveling
for a vodka soda?

In the words of someone wise:
It doesn't get better, it gets WORSE.

It seems @FedEx has lost
some priceless items of mine.
I don't understand how a
$60 billion company can have
no idea what is going on with a package.
Rude.

@UPS, y'all looking for a brand ambassador?

Iconic behavior:
me arriving to Twitter once every five months.
Alright, I think that's enough Twitter for the decade.
I bow to the artistry.

Source: @VioletChachki

Mrs. Kasha Davis Finds Enlightenment Under a Tree

I'm sending you love tonight
and smiles before bed.
I'm Polly Positivity.
Truth!

THIS is serenity,
accepting this moment,
the light, cool air and just being together.

I'm so excited about 2022!
I know times are ridiculously tough
and it can be a very melancholy day,
but for a moment,
please accept our love and hope for good health,
happiness, and abundance
this day and upcoming year!

When you walk past a mirror,
give yourself a smile
and a THUMBS UP!
You deserve it!

Getting older is FABULOUS!
We grow, learn, and have a valuable
treasure chest of experiences to reflect upon.

Performing in drag has been
an incredible way to share positivity and hope.
I could see myself doing drag till I'm 55.
After that, I'll open a coffee shop with my hubs.

I'm an "old bag,"
and you can buy my merch and smile too!
I'm always a text away.
Lots of love from our home to YOURS

Source: @KashaDavis

Kornbread Dreams
of Brighter Days to Come

It's Dick:35 pm somewhere!
Still time to let it free from the cages.
I'm so down to shake a titty.

This is porn. Messy ass
can't even be a ho in peace.
And I won't lie and say it's easy.

We just grade each other's
nudes to send to trade.
I'm screenshot-ting this.
Let's see the results tomorrow.
Lmfao I'mma still complain.

Just ate my last chicken tender for the next six months.
I actually used to get vegan before I started drag.
For three years. Got tons of evidence haha.

I wake up every day THANKFUL
I'm practically representing myself
and my best interest for my career.
Feels good to know I'm not being cheated.

Baby, I own my song lol.
This tweet with this song is so dramatic
and it's what we all need for breakfast.

Never let a bad thing block you
from happiness:
it happens to the best of us.
But if we don't move on we allow them to win.
Bitch, you on a roll.
That's how it's supposed to be!

Source: @kornbreadTMFS

Choriza May Wants to Be the Very Best, Like No One Ever Was

I've been accused of doing "womanface."
I think that's a very generous thing to say.
I have the kindest haters.
¡¡ME VOLÓ LA PELUCA!!

Oh no, Linda is judging my morals.
That's rich. Don't be like Linda.
Be nice to the queens who are on a show to entertain you.
You mad about someone's elimination?
Buy a ticket to their show, buy their merch,
send them a lovely message.
Why choose hate when there are
so many ways to share the love?!

Let's all block and report the haters.
¿No es mala idea eh?
Shut up, Linda.
¡ME CAGO EN TOS TUS MUERTOS!

¡Mis menos no importan,
hay que centrarse en lo positivo!
I just can't believe the amazing things
I got to experience over the past few weeks.
I am so, so thankful.

Oh, wait?!
A *Pokémon* game based in Spain?
And you didn't expect me to get involved?
I feel like there is not a single gay person
working at Nintendo.
Some of these Pokémon are so bad.

COMING SOON:
MONSTERADOR. The Corrida Pokemon!
RORCHAIGER. The Ink Pokémon!
TAUROS (Regional Form). The Bull Pokémon!
APHROWLDITE. The Revenge Pokémon!
ANJIZA. The Abundance Pokémon!
GENZAIDON. The Light Pokémon!

Did you enjoy my SV Elite Team?
¿Jugaremos juntas cuando saquen el juego porfa?
I can't wait to see you, mi amor!

Time to say goodbye to my beard until April 2023.
A no te preocupes que me ha hecho muchísima gracia.

Source: @chorizamay

Bosco Tightens Her Corset
for the Buffet

The things I do to make twelve year olds
stop calling me poor on the internet.
OH SO WE HAVE JOKES.
We are choosing violence today, I see.

Which one of you gays
is in charge of this account????
Bury that whore then.
I am literally demanding
capital punishment for you.

To the tune of "Creep" by Radiohead:

It had to be said:
THIS LOOK RULES.
Literally invented rhinestones.
THEY LOOK SO GOOD ON YOU.

Oh we felt like pressing
the slay button tonight.

I am here representing the
demographic of slutty bullies,
I regret nothing, and I would do it all again.
I'm a loser! I'm incredibly loose.

I'm glad we are both members of
the "skinny bitches with cute dumpers" club.
The only thing missing was estrogen TBH.
Just kidding, they are sold out

This has been a magical day.
Maybe March is for women

Source: @hereisbosco

Maddy Morphosis Avoids Typecasting with a Serpentine Movement

I'm very fortunate to be in the position I'm in,
and to have the platform that I've been given.
And this month I want to take this opportunity
and be make some kind of direct
and positive change within the community:

My new drag name is Wonderbread.
Did you want that glamour original or extra crispy?

Nothing beats cracking a cold one
and watching X-Games with my sis.
Just guys bein' dudes.
Go team! Go sports!

I didn't realize how many people were just
chilling out there,
lol I was not at my most flattering.

I started drag right around the time
my hairline started to recede.
Now I wear fake hair for a living.
If that's not fate, idk what is.

Wounds have healed, we're good now.
We better stop before people think
we're actually fighting
and post us on the drama subreddits
Thank you for coming to my defense.

Anyway, back to shit-posting.
Not Taylor Dayne liking this lol.
One last twist of the knife

Source: @MaddyMorphosis

A'keria C. Davenport
Goes for the Emmy

Good morning.
It's a beautiful day in the gayborhood!

I had a full on *Pose* moment in WeHo last night.
As I'm walking with some friend,
I ran into a young black group of gays and a trans girl...
they were in their own element but saw me
and was saying how they look up to me...
them living for me wasn't the highlight,
but to see the next generation being so free
at such an early age living their truth
really made my night.

Girl, I'm really an "auntie" now,
but it feels good.

Anyone can shine in the light,
but watch me GLOW
through any darkness!
It's giving superhero.

Even on my chill shiiiit
I'm the hottest in the room!

I lost a bag, I got bigger ones.
I lose some "friends," I got realer ones.
I took some L's, I turned them into Lessons.

I never lack, I only transition.
My life in a nutshell.
Let the church say AMEN.

Source: @A_doubleC_D

Tatianna Accepts a Lifetime Achievement Award in Choices

Am I about to enter my wifey era?
I'm hanging in there, lol.
This bitch is embarrassing.

So I decided to watch the *Bratz* movie
while I rhinestone one of my costumes this morning,
and I completely forgot how insanely bad this movie was.
I mean, I'm still gonna watch it,
but damn.
What the absolute fuck?!

I always flip off the people protesting
the abortion clinic by my house
when I drive by,
but today I wasn't paying attention
and flipped off three innocent ladies
standing at the bus stop.

At this point I feel like Kanye
is just upset that he isn't the one with Pete.
Just heard someone say Kanye has the emotions
of a goth kid who just got broken up
with by the person who give him his first kiss.
Absofuckinglutely. Very that!

Let's focus on what BRITNEY wants to focus on.
Britney woke up and chose violence today,
and I fully support that.
This is AMAZING!
Whew, this mess just keeps getting messier and messier.

Today ended up being a real eh.
Unrelated, but I'm also very tired.
Better luck tomorrow.

Source: @TATIANNANOW

Willam Belli In the Universe Where She Got the Villain Edit

I am nasty at times.
Thank God we have Twitter so
u can remind the 1,101 people
that care what u think.
Tag me, bitch.

Didn't you all learn nothing from 2018?
That was when Karens were fun.
Your memory has failed u.
Fight me. I ain't wrong.

Comparison is the thief of joy.
Stop trying to diminish someone's accomplishments.
Why not just enjoy us for what we are?

Speaking of "not a good look:"
your whole fucking page, TBH.
The cringe on your Twitter takes on ageism
re: Sarandon, transphobia, hating on Lin-Manuel Miranda.
I don't care to have you in my orbit.
Ride, Sally Ride almost off the planet...
You rotten, rotted man.

Wi-Fi + opinions = podcast.
U should get one.

Hahahaha FUCK.
That was so fun.
Now all's I need is a VCR.
Lemme get some of those Cheetos too.
Also need someone to do a 3D scan of my face.

Due to the sickening nature of COVID,
this is a wrap on the holiday tour.
You can't erase me but keep trying.
I'm popular.
Be back soon, I hope.

Source: @willam

Blu Hydrangea Reveals Her Rusted Nail

Yesterday, I posted a hate message I received,
and someone replied 'keep your chins up.'

Thank you, love.

You'd be unbearable if you got on
that show for more than a few seconds.

Don't take out your age insecurities on me.
We see your negative comments, so be nice.
The people you may have "lost" as fans,
you probably didn't want in the first place!!!!

They should have an option to hide subscribed blue ticks.

When you meet a queen who uses Facetune, they look different.
But, when you meet a queen who uses FaceApp...
who did this photo even start off as?

Wait, you're being nice?
Oh, was this a compliment?
Sometimes, I just come to
the comment section with my guard up.
I did feel really pretty.

I mean, I'm also incredible at what I do,
but I do love drag and intake it in any form I can.
Drag Race has given me the opportunity
to buy a house before I'm 30.
I'm ok, babe.

I'm sorry, Crystal.
Idk how my dildo got on your set.
It's such a Northern Irish thing;
do a shot every time she does it.

Sorry I was steaming.
I'm a little drunk,
and this was a sensory overload.

*Source: @BluHydrangea_*

Jasmine Kennedie Goes Supernova, Leaves No Survivors

Feeling on top of the world!
A year and some estrogen
does a body good!!!
This makes me smile extra big.

I get to live my *Showgirls* fantasy!!!
Nomi Malone step aside,
my titties will be playing a
role in this upcoming endeavor.

I feel my voice isn't loud enough
and can still get a little bigger.
They can't fit all my talking in.
Y'all are really testing my limits today.

H&M showroom is a little different
than off-the-rack H&M.
Giving you Wanda and Cosmo fantasy.

My lower back is fine,
thank y'all for asking.
You gotta let the people
know when you're a power bottom.
You already knowww.

Thank you all for the amazing support!!!
Y'all are the fucking best ever!!!
The amount of love and support over
the last couple of days has been amazing.
I love my bimbos!

Source: @jasminekennedie

Heidi N. Closet Gives a Talking Head During an Eclipse

Good morning, beautiful people.
Question of the day: What's your biggest turn off???
I'll go first!!!!
A nasty personality, that'll do it for me...

I go everywhere and hear
bad behavior stories all the time!!!
Literally in the last three days,
I've heard two stories of different queens
and I'm just like, "Well we aren't all like that."

The way I just ran across this airport...
Omg.
Woke up at 3:30 so I could pack
to leave my hotel at 4:30,
boarded plane at 6:40 to take off
at 7:20...
it's now 9:18 and we still on the ground.
Get it together.
I almost threw my phone at the airport.

Since I'm headed to the UK,
I definitely packed my Burberry outfit
and plan on wearing to the Burberry store.
Girl, it's going to be a good time.

Just realized my phone was muted,
no wonder I haven't been
getting my notifications.
Iconic moment.
Everything happens for a reason.

Wishing everyone a
blessed and highly favored day.
I'll be sure to tag you next time lol.

Source: @HeidiNCloset

Willow Pill, The Morning After...

Hello, my children.
Welcome to Willow's World!
I quit drag!
Today is the day, y'all!
Y'all asked, and you shall receive!

I just walked into an important appointment
and said, "so sorry I'm late, I had a personal emergency!"
with my hair freshly dyed and
a hot pink Ulta bag in my hand.
She's a comedienne.

I was going through my room today
and found this picture of RuPaul
I kept pinned to the wall of my hotel room
during filming to remind me she's human like me.
Can someone edit this
so my eyes are lasering into her ass?
I'll kiss you.

The only person's opinion I care about:
Luther Vandross.
He has my number.
Let's spend eternity in Hell.
I love you, my baby!
A thousand kisses from
you is never too much.

I'm so proud of my win,
but I definitely had an advantage
not having to cosplay as a Republican.
Y'all adult gays sending hate to
a 21-year-old living their dream
on *Drag Race* because you didn't
love their outfit is so weird.
Like, look at yourself in the mirror
and maybe cry a little bit.

Remember, there are almost
a million people on the planet,
and each and every one of you is special!

Hold on,
I'm being informed there are
seven billion people.
I take this back!

Whatever happens tonight,
we're all ugly.
Love you babe!!!!!

Source: @WillowPillQueen

Adore Delano Sees the Face of God in a Pizza Grease Stain

I don't blame Cardi for deleting her socials.
This shit is yawn now.

Normalize wearing AirPods
in public spaces and pretending
you're in a music video.
Sometimes self-love is
wearing a face mask while playing Jewel.

I think we're gonna hop back on the health journey.
I think after six years of being vegetarian,
I'm going to try to become vegan.
I'll let you know how it's going in a month.
I ate my weight in carbs in the lounge before the flight
and now I'm munching on chips and pretzels.

I love memoirs—so far I've read Elvira's,
Drew Barrymore's, Miriam Margolyes',
Goldie Hawn's, Jewel's, and Jessica Simpson's...
I need to write a book soon.

I accept all pronouns:
He/she/they/them/Princess.

I always feel so bad when people
misgender me, 'specially when they're older.
I'm always like,
"no worries...sorry I'm a bad bitch..."

I live different lives each day,
so I want us all to feel
welcomed and safe at all times.

Wow. Me for president.
I'm crying.

Source: @AdoreDelano

Bianca Del Rio Gives a Masterclass in Front of a Dumpster Fire

A drag queen who can't successfully
complete a "meet and greet" is
A PIECE OF UNGRATEFUL SHIT!

If I see another "PROFESSIONAL"
DRAG QUEEN with DIRTY LACE and NO EARRINGS...
GIRRRRLLLLLL.

I love it when the ZIPPER
is working HARDER than
the DRAG QUEEN WEARING IT!

Have you washed your
makeup brushes today?
Washing your face helps.
I'm having trouble just figuring out YOUR FACE.
You really have no idea how any of this works......
DO YOU?

You should go NATURAL!
Just like ME!
XANAX makes me PLEASANT.
You should try the DRUGS!
LEARN, MY CHILD. LEARN.

I'm doing a concert at PRIMARK!
I think we can all agree...
WE DO NOT NEED ANOTHER COVER
OF SANTA BABY......
EVER!
Do your American pop culture research.

So, have y'all seen any good MEMES lately?
I wanna see them!
THANK YOU!

Source: @TheBiancaDelRio

Derrick Barry Nails His Theses to the Door of the Church of Britney

I'm so excited for this new
Britney Spears era.

Britney's voice is finally being heard
loud and clear all over the world.
Some pop stars never incorporate
a kick and/or splits,
but Britney Spears was out there
doing a high kick, with her left leg,
while pregnant with her second baby.

One of the many reasons
she'll remain my favorite.
Look how beautiful she was pregnant.

I hope Lifetime is finally rethinking
the Britney movie they made.
If Piers Morgan interviews Britney Spears,
hopefully he can start off with
an apology for being part of
the media problem in 2008,
which was also the year she was
put into a conservatorship.

I will always be #TeamBritney.
One day it will be your turn.

Success starts when
quitting is no longer an option.
Success is figuring out
a way to make money while you sleep.
I love my job.

Whenever I'm tired, feel like I can't perform
or need a day off, I remind myself
that I moved to Vegas when I was 20 years old
to perform six nights a week
in a six month contract.

Performing for a living is exactly
the life I wanted out of high school.
I'm still doing what I love.

Last night I fell asleep smiling
and it felt so good.
Try it.

Source: @DerrickBarry

Cheryl Hole Never Left.
She Was Always Here

SHE'S BACK!
I'm nervous, I'm excited, I'm READY!
I just slept for 15 hours uninterrupted,
and now I'm confused what year it is...
I'm honestly trying to pull myself out of bed
after my shows yesterday! My body is in bits.

Are you ready to dive into the
spookiest, scariest, and weirdest corners of the world?
Come get ready with me and
enjoy a cocktail, divas.
We're discussing the creepy case of
The Pizza Bomber and internet icon Slenderman.

Each week, we unpack some of craziest murders,
conspiracy theories, and ask all the questions!
This is now why my favorite Spice Girls era
was from May 31, 1998 to December 2000.

Nightclubs have ruined me,
yeah, I think my face says it all...
I just drew on my eyebrows on the train,
so if anyone sees me today, I apologize.

If I don't make it to London today,
just know I will die as I lived:
mediocre!

Thank you for always being by my side,
but more importantly,
thank you for putting up with
all my crap.

Source: @CherylHoleQueen

Trixie Mattel Before the Unveiling of Her Gold Statue

Good morning, you junkie whores.
Just like my pioneer ancestors, I'm hungover.
She had too much prop wine.

Alexa, play "Watercolor Eyes" by Lana Del Rey.

Just a young woman spreading joy and
her legs across the country on tour!
And speaking of legs,
everyone keeps trying to fuck me!

Does it ever end!?
We're halfway through the first leg
of our North American tour.

If you aren't bald, you can't come.
I'm sorry for any inconvenience.
Normalize being old, bald, and disgusting.

Alexa, play "Juice" by Lizzo.

STOP SENDING HATE TO DRAG QUEENS
that I don't already hate.
Maybe drag queens should start sending
death threats to fans.
Lol, people need to touch grass
and breathe and enjoy television.

Gays in their 30s...I can't.

Thanks everyone for your support.
Still saying this daily:
Everyone wants to fuck me,
and I totally get it.
I'm a young human girl in her prime!
If I don't do adult films, then who will?

Alexa, play "Brave" by Sara Bareilles.

Source: @trixiemattel

Jujubee Writes a Book to Read on the Toilet

I keep reminding myself that this journey
is so special and it's uniquely mine,
just like yours is yours.

I'm aging myself and not even mad about it!!!

Spilling the beans, because I'm old.
Gorgeous and old!
HEAD TO TOE BEAUTIFUL!!!

Great auntie in the streets...
daddy in the sheets.

It's has to be 1,000+ thread count sheets, though.
My skin is sensitive.

We've got dinner plans Tuesday!!!
Having a salad topped with sausage roll "croutons".
So excited!!!

It's going to be filled with trauma.

The peaks and valleys of life are
the best reminders that we own nothing.
Let's make the best of what we are given.

Keep moving. Be light. Be LOVE.
THIS IS HOW THE BEST LEMONADE IS MADE!!!

I can't wait to have supper with you...
but only if you wear a tracksuit.

Source: @jujuboston

Katya, Because Who Needs Context?

Ring in the new year with a lovely poem!

Have you heard the news?
I love Elisabeth Shue.

Sick on tour and mad as hell
Well...they got you, gals.

My two moods: joyful and XXX-tatic
We come to this place for magic.

Blazer on without my blouse,
that is how I leave the house.

Diva, you were serving hunty.
Did Jean Smart win the Emmy?

This is exactly the kind of energy I'm bringing into 2022.

The only Ryan Murphy project that I'm interested in
would be *American Wig Story Volume 1: Australian Wig Mystery*
and it's just about Nicole Kidman's wigs.
The wig alone is cruel and unusual punishment.
She ate, snapped and yeeted the wig into the lake!

Do you think Nicole Kidman is going to
win the best actress Oscar?
Academy voters, please, I beg you not to
overlook this performance by an
actress in a major motion picture.

There need to be way more roles
in movies for actresses in their fifties.
Are you a big old diva who lives to serve?
No one is doing it like you, Miss Laurie!

Getting ahead in Hollywood can be tough,
but it helps to have one foot in the door.
The length of my left foot is half an inch less
than that of my right foot.
Shout out to all my asymmetric divas
stuffing that one shoe with who knows what.

You know what's fierce?
Otters are causing seagrass plants to have more sex.
Work diva.

Source: @katya_zamo

Victoria Scone Serves an MRA's Head During Afternoon Tea

Before the next episode,
something for the sapphics.
Can't wait to piss off the misogynists more tonight xo.

Y'all know "fish" is a banned word
in the UK franchise of *Drag Race,* right?
Cast are categorically not allowed to say it.
The BBC recognizes this word's meaning.
You have a problem with "gatekeeping your language?"
CC the BBC.

Take note of the openly blatant misogyny
in the replies, comments, and public posts.
It's always been there.
Now they just have something mainstream enough
to say it loud about that you'll see it yourself.
Are you surprised? I'm not.

Funny thing is my drag performance
is pretty damn vulgar.
I talk proudly about my lived queer stereotypes,
my vagina, my weight on the regular,
because that's my lived experience to speak about.

That's why I'm saying it now...
on this tweet...
about myself...
not about anyone else's preferences...

Because...
checks notes
It's my vagina.

A lesbian in plaid?
Groundbreaking.
SORRY MOTHER JUST INVENTED MOTHERING!
HAHAHA!

My fans are the sexiest, just saying.
Everything reminds me of them.
We all kissed shortly after.
Let the showmance commence.

This would be such a camp house.
Imagine the karaoke nights.
Don't threaten me with a good time.

Source: @VictoriaScone

Bimini Bon-Boulash Perched Atop the Tower of London

People that use the British flag as
a symbol for their intolerable views
must forget what the 'union' Jack stood for.
My England is for everyone.
What does patriotism meant to you?
I wanna be inside EU.

I remember being attacked by
a group of football fans
for being visibly queer.
I was told I would make their children gay.
I hope the person's kids are gay
and I hope they're happy.

The last 18 months since the show
have been incredible, but I've encountered
so many snakes.
I've been sued, lied to, heartbroken
by people I thought were my friends.
People are fine with you until you start to succeed.

Grateful for my life and everything I get to do,
but it has come at a price. I'm in a place where
I'm happy now, but this year I have been
the unhappiest I've ever been.
I'm done with the fake people.
I'm gonna continue to do what I do,
and if you're real, then I'll fuck with you.

Hey, @MayorofLondon...
remember endorsing me as your successor?
Let's get the Tories out completely and
then get a plan in motion.
It's the era of embellishments, clashing,
and maximalism, baby.
Ready when you are!

Hahaha, love pissing people off.
Still I rise, and I'm just getting started.

Source: @biminibabes

Silky Nutmeg Ganache Hijacks the Airwaves

Are y'all not accustomed to black, queer people?
Y'all used TS Madison quotes
but didn't know who she was.

Y'all defending bullshit.
My black ass never said anything that crazy
to a queen on Season 11,
yet I was met with death threats.
The block thumb is strong today.

I have to go the extra mile and
other girls don't even have to go an inch???
Answer that. But answer with truth.

I love how whiteness is always supported.
Cry and the white fans will forgive.

Since so many of y'all are unbiased
and you don't see color,
the next time a black queen
reads a white girl,
be sure to say it's her unique humor,
she's making good tv,
or you just don't understand her.

I'm just a BIPOC that felt that jab.
But I'm used to it.
White queens, you can take BLM
off your name now,
the trend is over.

Today has been stressful.
I need wine and chorizo.
In that order.

We all got on *Drag Race* to
simply make our family proud
and create a new life for ourselves.

No matter how the fandom may react to us,
I'm sure every girl in all 14 seasons
wanted the same.
Give my sisters her flowers.

Source: @SilkyGanache

Kim Chi Ascends to a Higher Existence While at Chipotle

Hi,
I got unlimited Chipotle for a year.
How was your day?

Nothing relaxes me more than looking at
giant family size things at Costco
that I'll never buy.
Is that weird?
Worst part about being single is
never being able to purchase any pastries at Costco
because you'll never finish the whole thing
in time before it goes bad.

Oops, too late to work on my summer body.
I was working on my summer bod,
but cheese happened.
The times I've grabbed shredded cheese by finger full
and dust those bad boys in my mouth...

Working on my summer body for 2025.
Would I still be alive by then?

COVID 'bout to have more comebacks
than Blackpink at this rate.
CDC just told me, "It be like that sometimes."

Never fuck with a Korean woman in a beige coat
carrying a Louis Vuitton purse.
My next life, I'd like to come back as
one of those bitchy Korean girls with a YSL bag
who's so skinny, can drink shots after shots,
and consume everything on the heavy, rich restaurant menu
and still somehow stay little.
All of her friends are exactly the same way.
I don't like this universe :(

I love being ugly at home, alone.
I wanna make a fierce ass charcuterie board,
but I don't think I have enough friends to come eat it.
I don't really wanna have sex,
I just wanna feel the weight of someone on top of my body.
Is that too much to ask for?

Poutine not Putin.
This is a Canadian tweet.
You're welcome!
Venmo over $5,000 at your earliest convenience.

Y'all love Britney vs. Christina,
but won't give Shawn Mendes vs. Harry Styles a chance.
Let's take down all men.
Fans be like:
When Harry Styles wear a dress:
"yesss femme representation nonbinary boots the
groundbreaking house down
truly a celeb we need in these times."

When drag queens wear a dress:
TOOT OR BOOT.
St. Patrick's Day is straight people's Pride.

I thought of a really good tweet last night,
but passed out before I could tweet it and now
I don't remember what the tweet was.
A truly offensive tweet.
Being an adult is hard this week :(

Source: @KimChi_Chic

Acknowledgements

"A'keria C. Davenport Goes For the Emmy" was originally published in *Morning Fruit Magazine* (June 2022).

"Monet X. Change Records Five Podcasts at Once" and "Kandy Muse Sitting Alone in the Black Lodge" were originally published in *Fairy Piece Magazine* (June 2022).

"Farrah Moan Doesn't Highlight, She Emphasizes" and "Derrick Barry Nails His Theses to the Door of the Church of Britney" were originally published in *Sage Cigarettes* (June/July 2022). "Farrah Moan" was also one of *Sage Cigarettes*'s nominations for Best of the Net 2023.

"Trixie Mattel Before the Unveiling of Her Gold Statue" was originally published online in *New Note Poetry* (July 2022) and in the *New Note Poetry 2022 Anthology* (2023).

"Yuhua Hamasaki Finds a Genuine Designer Bag on a Table Full of Bootlegs," "Gottmik Inhales a Rainbow-Colored Fume," and "Tatianna Accepts a Lifetime Achievement Award in Choices" were originally published in *Indecent Magazine Issue 1* (August 2022).

"Bob the Drag Queen Gazes Into the Purse, and the Purse Gazes Also" originally appeared in *Stanza Cannon Issue 3* (September 2022) and *Cutbow Quarterly Issue 2* (December 2022).

"Maddy Morphosis Avoids Typecasting with a Serpentine Movement" was originally published in *The Creative Zine: Issue 4* (October 2022).

"Kornbread Dreams of Brighter Days to Come" was reprinted in *Bulb Culture Collective* (November 2022).

"Jasmine Kennedie Goes Supernova, Leaves No Survivors" was originally published in *Unstamatic* (November 2022).

"Kim Chi Ascends to a Higher Existence While At Chipotle" and "Katya, Because Who Needs Context?" were originally published in *Fifth Wheel*

Press (November 2022).

"Trinity the Tuck Pumps Up Her Spirit and Her Lips" and "Pandora Boxx After the Hinges Rust Off" were originally published in *Alice Says Go Fuck Yourself Issue 1* (November 2022).

"Aquaria Hits Shuffle on Her iPod Nano When the Molly Hits," "Bosco Tightens Her Corset for the Buffet," "Jujubee Writes a Book to Read on the Toilet," "Mo Heart Sets the Pulpit Alight with Just Her Voice," and "Shea Couleé Armors Up for Her Next Slaying" were originally published in *Dream Pop Press* (December 2022).

"Cheryl Hole Never Left. She Was Always Here" was originally published in *Red Ogre Review* (February 2023).

"Ginger Minj Licks a Glamour Toad and It Gets Weird" was originally published in *The Alien Buddha Gets Rejected: Part 2* (February 2023). "Heidi N. Closet Gives a Talking Head During an Eclipse" was reprinted in this issue.

"Violet Chachki: Portrait of a Bothered Queen" was reprinted in *Eunoia Review* (April 2023).

"Bianca Del Rio Gives a Masterclass in Front of a Dumpster Fire," "Laganja Estranja Discovers a New Color When the Chronic Hits," "Willam Belli In the Universe Where She Got the Villain Edit," "Adore Delano Sees the Face of God in a Pizza Grease Stain," and "Willow Pill, The Morning After..." were originally published in *The Gorko Gazette* (April 2023).

"Bimini Bon-Boulash Perched Atop the Tower of London," "The Vivienne Does a Tip Spot Outside 10 Downing Street," "Silky Nutmeg Ganache Hijacks the Airwaves," and "Blu Hydrangea Reveals Her Rusted Nail" were originally published in *Not Ghosts, But Spirits Vol. III* (2023).

Special Thanks

I would like to thank Emily Perkovich and Querencia Press for publishing this collection of poetry. I am so glad you took a chance on this absurd collection and for allowing me to share my centos with the world. I am so proud to now be part of the Querencia family.

I'd like to thank Kaylee Hernandez for her amazing cover art that has added the right amount of camp and joy to the look of this collection.

I'd like to thank the editorial staffs behind *Morning Fruit Magazine*, *Fairy Piece Magazine*, *Sage Cigarettes*, *New Note Poetry*, *Indecent Magazine*, *Stanza Cannon*, *Cutbow Quarterly*, *The Creative Zine*, *Unstamatic*, *Fifth Wheel Press*, *Alice Says Go Fuck Yourself*, *Dream Pop Press*, *Red Ogre Review*, *Alien Buddha Press*, and *The Gorko Gazette* for publishing earlier versions of the pieces in this collection. I'd also like to thank *Eunoia Review*, *Alien Buddha Press*, and *Bulb Culture Collective* for republishing pieces after the original site they were on was deleted.

I'd like to thank the forty queens in this collection whose honesty, humor, and creativity on Twitter lead to the creation of these poems. I'd also like to thank the other queens in the franchise, as even if I wasn't able to make a poem out of your posting histories, I still have the utmost respect and reverence for your art and boldness.

I'd like to thank Rachel Kurasz for being my best friend and an incredible creative partner, who gave me so much encouragement and support in this process. I'd like to thank the Thursday Night Poets group, including Robert Allen, Nolcha Fox, Tim Moder, Ken Tomaro, Molly Greer, Rorisang Moerane, and Stefanie Kirby for letting me share work from this collection and offering feedback and support.

I'd like to thank other writing groups and organizations I've been involved with, including Quail Bell Magazine, Cambridge Writers' Workshop, Split This Rock, Survival of the Fittest, Fifth Wheel Press, and Sage Cigarettes for their community spaces and resources. I'd like to thank nat raum, Raegen Petrucha, and Jesi Bender for providing blurbs for this collection. I'd also like to thank other writers for their support and encouragement, including Thaddeus Rutkowski, Nicole Tallman, tommy blake, Angela Caravan, Brina Patel, Katharine Blair, Sata Prescott, Archy Jamjun, Leah Angstman, Lori Hettler, Marlena Chertock, Joseph Lezz, Red Focks, Diana Norma Szokolyai, Rita Banerjee, Christine Sloan Stoddard, Katie Manning, Veronica Bennett, Raddy Gee, Camisha Jones, Rasha Abdulhadi, Addie Tsai, Charlene Elsby, Leza Cantoral, Christoph Paul, Greg Mania, and all the rest.

Naturally, I have to thank my family for their continued support and encouragement. If it weren't for my parents, Jenifer and Kevin, stepparents Jeff and Juliet, siblings Sam, Emily, Sean, and Evan, sister-in-law Christina, and the rest of my extended family reading *May All Our Pain Be Champagne* and encouraging me to top it somehow, this book may not exist.

I'd like to thank RuPaul, whose television franchise brought hundreds of queer entertainers to light and who changed me forever as a fan of reality television, as a bisexual man, and as a writer and poet. Thank you for all the memes, quotes, and references.

And finally, of course, I'd like to thank all the drag performers who don't have the platform or notoriety brought by the franchise, because it was seeing you all in small bars in Virginia and Washington DC that truly kept my love of the art of drag alive. Even though your art form is currently under threat, what you do matters greatly to so many people, and I deeply appreciate how much time and effort goes into honing your craft. You will all have your day in the sun, and I will be there handing you dollar bills in between sips of my bottomless mimosa.

About the Author

Alex Carrigan (he/him) is a Pushcart-nominated poet, editor, and critic from Alexandria, Virginia. His debut poetry chapbook, *May All Our Pain Be Champagne: A Collection of Real Housewives Twitter Poetry* (Alien Buddha Press, 2022), made the longlist for Perennial Press First Chapbook Awards. He has had fiction, poetry, and literary reviews published in *Quail Bell Magazine, Lambda Literary Review, Barrelhouse, Sage Cigarettes* (Best of the Net Nominee, 2023), *New Note Poetry, Jupiter Review, Whale Road Review, Bullshit Lit, Stories About Penises*' (Guts Publishing, 2019), and more. He is also the co-editor of *Please Welcome to the Stage...: A Drag Literary Anthology* with House of Lobsters Literary. For more information, visit https://carriganak.wordpress.com/ or follow him on Twitter @carriganak.

www.ingramcontent.com/pod-product-compliance
Lightning Source LLC
Chambersburg PA
CBHW071212120626
46546CB00006B/2520